Remember in Pieces

Linda H.Y. Hegland

Cyberwit.net
HIG 45 Kaushambi Kunj, Kalindipuram
Allahabad - 211011 (U.P.) India
http://www.cyberwit.net
Tel: +(91) 9415091004 +(91) (532) 2552257
E-mail: info@cyberwit.net

Copyright© 2022 Linda H.Y. Hegland
ISBN: 978-93-95224-19-2

First Edition: 2022
Rs. 200/-

Printed in India at VCORRE LLP.

Dedicated to my two sons,

Kelsey and Lindsay

Acknowledgements

'Greyhound Bus' appeared in the Taj Mahal Review - Volume 21, Number 2 Dec 2021

'Botany Trip' includes lyrics from 'Dust in the Wind' by Kansas

'Sweet, Sweet Burn of Summer' includes lyrics from 'Summer Fling by k.d. lang

'Wilding' makes mention of the book 'Wilding' by Isabella Tree

'Wilding' quotes a line from George Carlin

'Horses at Bozeman' includes lyrics from 'Wildfire' by Michael Martin Murphy

'Old Trucks and Prairie Songs' first appeared in Sky Island Journal Issue 1, Summer 2017

'Place of Ocean - Tides and Heartbeats' first appeared in 'Poetic Inquiry - Enchantment of Place', Vernon Press (Vernon Series in Art), Winter 2017

'Kissing Rabbits' first appeared in Sky Island Journal, Issue 5, Summer 2018

'Loving Monsters' first appeared in Sky Island Journal, Issue 7, Winter 2019

VIGNETTE (noun)

- a short descriptive literary sketch

- a brief incident or scene (as in a play or movie)

- tiny essays, postcards, little wisps of big ideas

- touchstone moments

VERSE (noun)

- a portion of a poem or song

- lines with rhythm of composition

Introduction

This is a book of vignettes and verses - remembered experiences, remembered conversations, remembered joys and regrets and shames and glory.

Life is messy.

Nothings lasts, nothing is finished, and nothing is perfect. This is true of both memory and life.

This all began when I started digitizing old photographs - photographs of my childhood, of my sons' childhood, of lived experiences. Each photo - old, ragged, foxed at the edges, faded . . . brought back memories. Made me nostalgic.

It is said that nostalgia is a form of 'homesickness'. I think, in these vignettes and verses, I am trying to find 'home'. Where the what and the who of me feels it belongs.

Contents

Two A.M.

It is two a.m. in the morning. I am up and wandering the upstair hallways, the ones in the peaks of the roof, shadows dogging at my heels, nudging at the edges of my sight.

The temperature is climbing and it is muggy. The night is almost silent. One lone cricket sings his mated dying song, sounding like that slow insistent beep in a hospital patient's room.

These nights where my mind wants me to remember - people, places, regrets, ecstasies - exhaust me.

No more the prairie girl that could dance all night until the pink of dawn in old, dusty barns at dances in places named Grassy or Black Diamond.

No more the night-long, cigarette-lit, wine-drenched conversations that went until the sun came up. The ones where you were falling in love, whether you knew it or not.

I used to sneak in the door just before my mother's alarm went off, make a pot of coffee, sit at the table and offer her a cup when she came in to the kitchen - as though I had woken just before her.

I have been a mother with sons of the same age as I was then. Sons who also danced and conversed with the long, long night. I know now I didn't have her fooled for one minute.

But now, the shadows still accompany me. Once and awhile the cat. I nurse a smoky whiskey and a fragile memory or two.

There is a quote I read somewhere that 3:00 a.m. knows all your secrets. I think that may be true. But I think 2:00 a.m. at least has an inkling.

Caution . . . Sharp Edges

I have edges
and there, where they meet,
are the shards of people that have broken on me;
have been cut by me.

I have left scars
and I keep scars of my own.
Catch your fingers on me and bleed;
best be careful of broken people.

Shred your shame on me,
shred your passion on me;
few things have such sharp edges
as my careless words.

Becoming takes a long time and
does not come easy to people
who break easy, or shatter fine.
I will leave you with more scar tissue than skin.

I hurt once too; hard,
like a hammer to steel.
My heart all in pieces, imperfect
and held in my hands.

You will not be carefully kept
with me; learn to deal
with the consequences
of a point too fine.

Linda H.Y. Hegland

I am dangerous.
Ground fine, jagged,
whetted . . . complex.
Caution . . . sharp edges.

Immigrants

Our first house in Canada was on a street of people from somewhere else. Out behind our house was prairie and horizon as far as the eye could see.

A dirt road, a scruffy street, peopled by immigrants from all over Europe - German, Italian, Ukranian, Spanish, Scandinavian, us English . . .

In the summer, we kids ran up and down the road in a multi-lingual tribe, with dogs and wagons with water and sandwiches in tow, playing until the single streetlight came on. That streetlight was home in a game of tag.

The houses were dilapidated, uninsulated, full of prairie dust. In the winter we wore our coats indoors.

My best friend was a little Italian girl from across the road whom I never did understand, nor she I. But we took our dolls and kittens and my dog down to the creek behind our place, under a stand of cottonwoods, and had tea parties - no language required.

My Mum birthed my brother, our labrador dog birthed 12 puppies and the cat birthed 6 kittens. All in the course of a full-moon week. The cat abandoned her kittens, ran away on the prairie, and the dog adopted them. Wee striped shapes amongst the burly wriggling puppyness.

One summer that dirt road was paved with hot tar and stones. I ran across the road shortly after the stinking tar machine moved up a bit and the soles of my feet burned, the skin on my soles coming away with the tar as is was peeled away from my feet. The rest of the summer my feet were wrapped in bandages.

As a result, I never won a game of tag that summer, too slow to the streetlight to call out 'Home!'

Silence Deafens

Silence deafens me.

Words and worlds alluded to,
silent shrugs, exaggerated sighs.
The cacophony near dogging me to despair,
compelling doubt; the spoken word,
the uttered word. Not to be trusted,
steeped in deceit, broken promises.
Conversations that strangle in the throat.

Silence deafens me.

The loud shout of it shuts my ears.
Reading the stories of my family
in still, haunted eyes;
in all things left unsaid.
I hoard these stories,
I clench the explanations,
I clasp the excuses.

I am the family storyteller.
I witness as an adult, bereft of a childhood.
I witness as a child, bereft of understanding.
Silence speaks volumes, speaks true and real.
Told in gestures and looks askance;
the tight-lipped grimace
of a word almost said.

I am the family storyteller and
my silence is bought and paid for.
Stories I tell in waterfalls of words,
hidden in the white noise.
The loudness of deep quiet reverberates in the echo
of my word-laden soul.
And the silence has deafened me.

Circle Dancing

It is the early hours of a blustery morning, about 3:30 am. I sit in the dark. The windows shake with each gust and the house squats down around me like a hen on its chicks. This tempestuous wind has kept me from finding sleep tonight. Instead, memories, those vague birds of observation, flutter around the edges of my mind. My senses thrum. The intonation of the wind in these wee hours is that of a low guttural stomp, stomp, stomp. Stomp, stomp, stomp.

The stomping sound of the wind takes me back to a prairie bar on a hot summer night, crowded with equally hot bodies in gingham shirts and fancy cowboy boots, doing a rhythmic circling two-step to the songs of Alabama or Emmy Lou Harris. That was actually not my 'thing' back then. But a friend had met a man who had a brother and, well, we paired up and all ended up going out together. It turned out that the brothers were Hutterite boys, members of an ethno-religious branch of Anabaptists who kept very much to themselves on the extensive communal colonies scattered throughout the prairies. These two were on their year away from the colony. A year when they get to try on the 'wild life', learn of its deviance and aberrance before returning to the commune, wiser and contented to stay.

They had initially lied about that, about being Hutterite. But they were not really like other boys we knew. We had guessed long before they told us. Their hair was slicked back with too much Brylcreem, their stiff brand new jeans were just that much too short, their breath smelled of cigarette smoke tinged with double mint gum. They were awkward and laughed too hard but had a strange, innocent bravado. They chewed that gum constantly, took it out when we kissed and fondled in the bed of their truck, and then popped it back in again. We only went out with them a half dozen times before they disappeared, presumably back to the colony, the world perhaps just a bit too worldly.

They insisted, each time they picked us up from the cafe near my friend's home because she was not supposed to be dating *at all*, that we go to the cowboy dance bar at the edge of a little town, just a short distance out of the city. A honky-tonk - wild, a little dangerous. Frequented by bikers and cowboys, both real and 'city' ones. Out there on the grassy prairie, the bar was a sweltering dark shadow under a moon-full sky; a few strands of year-round Christmas lights draped around the door and around the 'Him' and 'Her' outhouses. Another around the wood-carved sign that simply said 'Bar'. The air was filled with the chirping of grasshoppers and the lazy on/off lights of fireflies.

A woman sat at a table at the door, selling drink tickets and checking ID. She didn't really check ID, though. We girls were sixteen and looked it. Instead, she stuffed a couple of extra drink tickets in our hands and winked. Grinned her near toothless grin. She was in her seventies, maybe eighties. She was called Aunt Sass. Her hair was a bright unnatural yellow and curled upwards in an elaborate cake-top bouffant. She wore a sequinned tank top from which her scrawny, wrinkled arms protruded like branches on a dying tree, and in which her breasts dived to her waist. Her jeans strained over a pot belly.

But she had the most beautiful boots, inlaid with turquoise and tooled elaborately all up and down the leather. Hummingbirds hovered on each toe, turquoise eyes eye-lidded with a sliver of opal. The heels stomped deliciously. She would sit, drinking rye whiskey and water, one after the other, until someone eventually asked her to dance or, if not, she would dance by herself. Our Hutterite boys were afraid of her. They skirted widely around her, bumping into tables and people, not meeting her eyes. She'd just chuckle and hoist her breasts.

Inside, the bar was dark as a pocket and the smoke was thick and choking. The smell of beer was pervasive, steeped like tea in the old plank floor, woven into the fibre of the carpeting under the tables. The boys liked this bar in particular because they served a pot luck dinner. Perhaps the motion of people filling plates and gathering around the small, nicked and gouged wooden tables reminded them of the communal meals back in the colony. They had hearty appetites and refilled their plates two or three times. We said to them that a potluck implied that everyone brought something to contribute to the table.

"Well, yeah, the women", was the reply.

These boys could not hold their liquor. Throughout the evening their cheeks would get rosier and rosier, their eyes brighter. They would look at each other and giggle like girls. The arm draped across my shoulders would get heavier, the shirt sweatier. Their dance steps became stumbled and addled. My friend and I knew that *we* would be driving their truck back to the motel where they stayed and that she and I would then be walking that dark highway back to the city. We stuck carefully to the shoulder, holding tight to each other when a semi-trailer blew by. In the dark, we would occasionally stumble on something heavy and soft, tripping over it, continuing on, trying hard not to think about what creature the roadkill was.

But up until then, all night long, we danced. Two-steps and cuddle-pivots, cowboy waltzes and circle dances. To the music, couples swirled round and round, as if in a rapture. I thought it was hokey, I certainly didn't like all of the songs. But nonetheless I found myself in that parade of shuffling, cowboy booted, damp and half-drunk couples going round and round. It was almost like a forced march, almost like we couldn't stop. Trance stepping. Stone-faced, sometimes singing along. Mesmerized by the measured stepping and swaying tempo. Hands held by sweaty hands. The smell of double mint gum panted down my neck. Stomp, stomp, stomp. Stomp, stomp, stomp.

Moon

I thought I could catch the moon;
throw a noose and pull it from the sky,
arms aching, breathless,
and it would light my world.

I thought I could follow the moon
along those beams it drops to the ground;
along the shores of seas;
along the earths own veins.

I thought I could swallow the moon;
hold it in my mouth, push it to my gut;
my stomach full with it,
and it would light my soul.

I thought the moon would love me back;
hold me in its alabaster arms,
cool fingers down heated back;
kiss my eyelids asleep.

But full moon to eyelash crescent;
just another star in my dark night,
just another space between my breaths,
turns a cold shoulder and leaves.

High School Prom

It is high school prom season. Fancy dresses and corsages and boys in suits for the very first time.

I never had any intention on going to my prom. I cared about a lot of things in high school, I really did, but prom wasn't even close. I hated the idea of all that parading (the 'promenading'), the leering grins around the spiked punch, the whispered dissing of various girls' choice of 'frock' behind cupped hands in the washroom, the making of the king and queen nomination list. The whole awkward display of it. It was so unlike me and so unlike my personality that the thought of it made me sneer and shudder in turn.

But my parents had other ideas, insisting that I attend this night of 'transition' - turning from child to adult in the course of a balloon-filled night. I felt I was adult enough already. I had been working in one form or another since I was thirteen. I was paving my own way to university without anyone's help - my family was disinterested. My boyfriend was from the opposing school, on the 'wrong' side of town, long-haired and poor (though a really great quarterback) and I had already learned about having drinks thrown on me for cheering for the other school's football team and other nonsense, hate-filled experiences.

In any event, I went - after suggestion became begging became insistence. My divorced mother spent money she didn't have on buying me a dress. Not fancy by any stretch of the imagination but a dress (I lived in jeans and sandals), pale-coloured and long. She also paid for an 'up-do', hauling my waist-long hair up into a sculpted and lacquered style that weighed on my head like a stone. My father paid for photos. My boyfriend wore an old suit of his fathers'. The sleeves of the jacket and legs of the pants were pinned under with barely discrete safety pins but I loved him for making the effort. He also had bought me a lovely, simple corsage of a single, white orchid. As we were going out of the door my father presented me with his other contribution to my 'coming out' - a big blousy purple corsage with which he replaced the one my boyfriend gave me. I slipped the white orchid into my purse.

The first part of the evening was for the parents. They lined the sides of the gymnasium to watch their offspring parade into the room - swishing dresses and pressed suits, to a song I don't remember but was probably reminiscent of a president's march. The first dance was supposed to be by the couples, viewed fondly by their parents on the sidelines. But for me . . . Well, my father, my Da' - who had taught to waltz by having me stand on his feet while he held me in a proper waltz pose and shuffled and turned me about the slippery linoleum kitchen floor when I was seven. And had taught me to dance the twist and how to jive. My Da' elbowed my boyfriend out of the way and waltzed me around the gymnasium with great swoops and dips - to my complete mortification.

We left the prom before the final dance (as my boyfriend had been told by a few of the football team that we would be met in the parking lot and he would get a good beating, being from that 'other' school and all. We took them seriously - they had done it before). I had slipped into the gym shower and washed all the junk from my hair and the makeup from my face and I changed into jeans, a t-shirt, and sandals I had stashed in my locker the day before. I pinned the white orchid into my hair. Then we snuck out and into my 1964 Corvair (a 16th birthday present from my father, a veritable death-trap) and drove two hours to Calgary. For coffee. And then drove two hours back again, music blaring out of the open windows; arriving back just in time for my job at the library early on that Saturday morning.

Can't tell you what happened to that dress. Can't tell you whether the king and the queen of the prom went on to equally beautiful lives.

Can't tell you what happened to my boyfriend, who I broke up with about a year later and completely broke his heart. He never, ever, forgave me. I *can* tell you that white orchids wilt quickly in the prairie heat of a June night. And that coffee you drive two hours for is no better than any other.

Leaving Me

How to find the important whispers?
The ones that are spoken across a room,
across a relationship;
the ones that are really
not meant to be heard.

You have begun to leave me,
in small steps and in small ways.
That thing you forgot to tell me,
that moment you forgot to share;
the stories you tell yourself,
and chuckle,
but don't let me in on the joke.

The whispers that tell the secrets,
tell the truth, tell the thing
I don't want to hear;
in one ear and out the other,
out of one's grasp.

You have begun to leave me.
Your eyes don't meet mine,
you smile at someone beyond
my shoulder, your arms
hug only yourself.
You don't stroke my hair
anymore.

The important whispers,
the ones that mean something,
the ones that hurt;
told in the subtext of
a love gone wrong.

Green Light

This morning, out of the bedroom window, fresh-washed by rain overnight, the world appears sea-green. The milky clear/not clear green of a watery world that is the home to seahorses and fish that carry their own lanterns. Any moment I expect transparent, undulant jellyfish to dance pirouettes past the window. In silence. In the green light.

Bomb Shelter

The school desk - a bomb shelter
of my generation. Spectre of a
Cold War and a cold war, indeed,
as it chilled the heart, the ice raising
goose bumps on the arms,
the cold trickle of fear down the back
like ice water; a breath hard to catch.

The practice drills called by the wailing
and howling of sirens like a
wolf at the moon;
that call to hide beneath those desks
to save ourselves though it was not hard
to imagine my small shape drawn like a
charcoal drawing on the institution-yellow wall -
grey ash, incinerated dust.

My friend's father built a real bomb shelter,
deep, deep in his back yard,
behind the magnolia tree and under the pines.
And she and I played hide and seek and I
hid in it, imagining falling bombs like the one
my mother told me of that fell in her bedroom
and took her eyebrows from her in
a war before this.

And while hiding there in that silent concrete,
listening to my friend calling my name out behind the magnolia,
under the pines, I would make note of the folded

blankets; the chess game with one pawn missing; count the rows and rows of cans of tomatoes and cans of soup; and make note, too, that there was no can opener.

Prairie Hair Salon

A friend posted on Facebook a lovely little story about Alastrina's hair salon in Greece and about how one sits outside to have one's hair cut amongst the bougainvillea and sun. I love the piece in and of itself but it also brought to mind . . .

When my boys were small and Bar and I were students and we were poor as poor, each of them - each son and my husband - would perch in turn on a stool in our prairie back yard and I would trim their hair. Out beside the laundry line. We did not have bougainvillea but we had the heady scent of lilacs and the heavy, sweet yellow of the caragana bushes.

The sun was hot and the scissors were huge, meant for cutting fabric, not tender blonde and red hairs. And the grasshoppers leapt onto my sons' dangling, dusty feet and up into the seams of my husband's jeans. Out through the doors music was playing, and loud. Probably something like Turley Richard's "When I Heard the Voice of Jesus'. The ever-constant wind blew the cut strands of hair out onto the prairie, out to the horizon.

Greyhound Bus

Here I go again -
riding on a greyhound bus
with dirty windows.
The man with the beard
sits much too close and the woman
in the front with her hymn book
open on her lap, her knitting
bag beside her, sings
much too loud and off-key.

The egg-salad smell
is there to stay in the
still stifled air of the bus.
At the stops along the way,
in worn out truck stops or
too-bright gas stations,
the only sandwich options are
egg salad or egg salad.

Coffee in those places is
always much too cold, the
smell bitter and burnt.
A burnt smell, too,
lifts from the bus tires
as the brakes whisper tired
rhythms with the rain
through the dark night.

Each time I do this I ache

for home,
my heart broken wide;
but here I am again,
on a greyhound bus
with dirty windows.

My breathe chokes
on egg salad and cold burnt coffee.
The sound of those whispering tires is
like a fine sharp wire through my head,
piercing. I can't think. I
can't feel. Anything. Anymore.
At some point
I sing along with the woman
and her hymns, page 16.

Old Wharf

I stand out at the end of an old decrepit wharf. It feels melancholy. Though she wasn't actually there, I could see a French lieutenants's woman sort of figure; waiting, longing, at the end of the wharf just where the fog hung.

And how she stared off at the horizon, the horizon where the sky is stitched to the ocean; a long line of sutures that keeps the world from falling apart.

And keeps us from falling off into those places where, on ancient maps, we were told 'there be monsters'.

And keeps at bay those glinthawks - that green flash on the sutured horizon at sunset or sunrise.

Those times of our unbelieving.

No wonder sailors go mad.

Time at Bay

At the edge of the ocean,
meditating on time playing
word games with myself on the
contrapuntal music of time –
infinity, lifetime, moon counting,
lastingness, season, eternity,
moment, tempo, day, night,
past, future . . . tide.

Children blur by me,
bolting from wave to shore,
from shore to stone;
tail-gating, bent to a destination.
I ricochet off the current they cause
like a mote of dust in the wind;
my time is slow to their fast,
another dimension – unseen.

Old man lumbers past in a suit
soaked with salt water,
he carries an old briefcase
of rusty cracked leather.
His salt-rimed face carries the musings and
ruinations in his mind, his lips
muttering arguments with himself;
he takes the time to think fully on them.

Cut Flowers

I will sing to you through the window, said the willow to the cut flowers. Until, on that one high note, you will remember what it was to be wild on those hot, rocky slopes of Turkey. When it was the wind that sang the spiralling note.

Kayak in the Bay

Lonely foggy morning,
seabird on the pier, head tucked.
Blue of mountain above blue
of water; purple smudge
at their meeting.
Kayak paddle to ocean swell;
wild geese on the horizon.
I watch the wet face of the water
beneath my paddle and indulge
in conscious reflection and subconscious dreams.
The water flows beneath me with each stroke;
the water flows through me with each caress;
vibrates and sings in aching muscle and sinew.
The kayak cleaves the curdled fog,
the paddle heaves with metronome rhythm.
I peer at rocks below,
green-dressed and barnacle-scabbed.
I invite the water, cold and salty,
to weep through my fingers;
invite the belonging.
When next I paddle, I will be alone, solitary.
When next I paddle it will be dusk, near dark.
I want to see the stars in the sky held below me in the water;
and believe, with all my heart,
that I am paddling the swell of the Milky Way.

First Open Window

The first open window to the night.

And the breeze, which in the winter is a shoving gale pitifully moaning at the window to be let in, tickles in at the opening. It stirs the drifting cobwebs in the peaks of the ceiling, the peaks of the roof, so high I don't see them In the light of day. It rocks the spider in the web like a baby in a cradle. It stirs the leaves on the potted lemon tree.

In the open window to the night, peepers sing 'til all hours; or until their steady, rhythmic chirr of a lullaby has sent me to sleep on that last rising note.

In the open window to the night, the moon's long light creeps over the sill. Kisses eyelids; caresses a brow; leaves moon pearls on cheeks.

And at the open window at early light, the window that frames the bone-stick branches of the Black Locusts, just coming into leaf, always last to come into leaf, the cat and dog gather. To listen to the morning nickers of Nancy, the white horse, as she greets the light; as she greets the red-winged blackbird; there in the blueberry field. Listened to from our window; the first open window to the night.

Questions at Night

A night of wakefulness alternately with
        deep, deep sleep.

Questions *just* there, just *there*,
        answers never quite grasped.

And sometimes the answers are so
        very, very simple.

Once a dragonfly settled next to me
        on a warm stone for an hour,

and the shimmering portal between us thinned,
        and I touched an elemental place.

And, sometimes, it is just the sheer,
        unutterable reverence of it all.

Treasure Boxes

A friend told me a most wondrous story. The story was about how he played the Russian anthem on a piano on the street. And how a woman who was from Russia was moved to tears and felt 'at home'. The story is much more involved than that, especially in light of wars and people. But it was the ending of the story that stayed with me. At the end of the story he said "Our beautiful world is not meant to be broken". That is what was written on that piano on that street - "Our beautiful world is not meant to be broken".

Since I heard it, this phrase has been wheeling in my mind. I will be reading a book and the phrase quietly enters my mind between lines in the story. I will be traipsing with fresh water out to the chicken coop and the phrase becomes a tune syncopated by my footfalls. I sing it to myself. I purr the words to myself as I listen to the news. Obviously, the phrase has become an emotional touchstone.

I will put it in a journal I have - leather-covered, faded and fat with pieces of paper shoved in, little scraps of maybe songs, pressed flowers, old letters, a drawing of me and my boys from a kind friend and reams and reams of quotes read or heard that I am frightened I will lose if they don't get put into this book. Kind of like a treasure box.

When I was a child I had a treasure box - an old shoe box that had once held my father's police boots. I kept it under my bed. It contained things I was frightened I would lose too. In it, the worn leather collar of my first puppy. The dried fragile body of a butterfly with only one wing. A single pearl from my mother's broken strand. A pair of eyeglasses with a crack across the lens (I do not know whose). A heavy, steely marble I won off of the cheating bully up the road. The amber eyes of the teddy bear I had since a baby; kept after he finally faded away, nothing left of him but burlap and the little scrap of leather that was his nose. My brother's yo-yo (I stole it) and my baby ring engraved with my name and birthdate and 'protect'. One of my mother's cigarettes and the heavy metal shoe token from a game of Monopoly.

All of those things are gone now, of course. But I still remember what I held in that box, I didn't lose them altogether. And now my over-stuffed old journal where, on a page all by itself written in purple ink, so I don't lose it, is "Our beautiful world is not meant to be broken".

Rain

Rain
 slithers . . .
down the sheen, the slick
of the window pane,
as grey wisps – cloud clots,
gather on bleak, stripped boughs;
like torn wool from sheep
on barbed wire fences.

Outside,
 bird . . .
drowned of song,
wings disheveled,
heart surging like
ocean-wrought waves,
sorrows, and fluffs feathers
under drenched leaves.

Flower,
 closed petals . . .
she was not urged to open
by her ardent sun
this blanched and anemic morning.
Sulking like a shut-in maiden;
invalid, damp and pale
in her bemired and bespattered bed.

Saunas

There is a sauna. Hand-built, a stove as hot as the hinges of hell. And always, always one or two or more cats piled on the splintered porch of it. It has an ante-room where one can disrobe and robe again. Where one can have a swig or two of beer or cider between searing douses of steam. It belongs to dear friends, old friends, that we have known for years and years and years. This sauna is in Ontario; our friends live in Ontario now.

But when we first met them it was when we all lived on the prairies. They had a farmhouse out beyond the edge of town. Nearby was a whiskey distillery and the air out there always had a bit of sour mash funk about it. And we always had an air of mild drunk about *us* as a result. They built a sauna out in a field on the edge of the horse pond. It was little more than a shack - just enough room for us four adults. And sometimes one of our small boys in a plastic baby bath filled with cool water that turned warmer and warmer and made them sleepy. Remembering a womb.

It had a stove more wicked than their current one. It glowed so red we hardly needed the candles we used to light the sauna. The steam was so hot it clouded our vision. The air felt thick and syrupy. Close. You could feel it surge into your lungs and back out again. Saunas are a peaceful, secret place to weep. Tears can drip with sweat down onto the wet musty floor. No one notices.

Between blasts of skin-peeling heat we would run to the horse pond. The ground around the pond was thick, churned mud and slime where the horses had come to drink. You had to be committed to running and jumping into the water. If not, you simply fell on your face in the mud. Once in the water, the feel of long grasses swaying against shins;

fish nibbling at ribs. The reflection of the stars in the water was like the Milky Way had fallen into it.

One night, full moon, and the horses were herding close to the sauna, restless. Occasionally they would peek in at us through the cloudy glass of the one narrow window. They made it difficult to leave and re-enter the sauna, crowding close, pulling wet hair and nuzzling naked shoulders. So we hung about outside the sauna to cool, not bothering with the pond, staring up at that gorged and extravagant moon. You could see the craters.

And, then, at one point we looked out to the field and one of our friends was sitting astride one of the horses. A spectral light upon a snorting shadow. His body glowed silver in the moonlight and great wafts of steam rose off of him like the steam from horses' nostrils in the winter. And, just for a moment, the grasshoppers stopped chirring and the moon somewhat wobbled. Just for a moment.

Our friends have a lovely sauna, the one they have now, with clean lines and amenities. But the sauna I love best is that one on the prairie; the one my sons fell to sleep in; the one I could weep in; the one of horses that throng; the one of steaming beings that stop the moon. With a pond of swaying grasses and curious fish.

Layers

One of those things that
wakes you up at 3:00 am
and keeps nudging at your mind
again and again until you fall back asleep.
I was thinking about layers.

About what you get to when you start
peeling all the layers of a memory.
About how when you peel layers of artichokes
you get to a heart, soft and tender.
And about how when you peel layers of onions,

you get to . . . nothing.
That's probably why onions make you cry.

Fog

This morning is draped in fog.

Trees, even those that have started to leaf, return to skeletal shapes, bony silhouettes.

The fog drifts down the mountain like curtains drawn across a stage; a hand across the eyes.

Pete's cows are lowing, their voices loud and unseen in the grey, grey, grey - like a fog horn.

When I was 10, a librarian (whose name I have long forgotten) gave me the gift of a book. The book was a collection of short stories by Ray Bradbury. I loved that book so much. When that copy wore out, I bought another of it in high school, and when that wore out, I bought another in university, and then another.

One of the stories in that book was 'The Fog Horn'. It was about a man who decided to make a sound, a voice to warn ships and sailors. But the voice was heard by a monster far out in the sea. A monster all alone and lonely - so very, very lonely and he comes to the lighthouse in search of a mate, in search of that other. Perhaps like our OgoPogo or the Loch Ness Monster.

Perhaps like ourselves.

Things Found at an Old Farm Sale

Things found at an old farm sale . . .

A box of keys,
rusted and filigreed;
doors long ago opened or locked;
and a nail that held together a house.

A box of books
damp and foxed; in one
a wordless meadow of
pressed flowers and dance memories.

A photo of a long-ago family
stern and black and white;
their lives long gone, the memories
sold for a dime.

An old bicycle with flaking paint,
a place for a lover on the handlebars;
a milk can smelling of warm bodies, damp
manure, and the heavy wetness of milk.

An old ring, muted gold,
a nick in the metal and a
flaw in the stone;
the inscription reads 'Devotion'.

Chief

I had a horse once. Named Chief . My father won him for me in a poker game. We kept him out on the place of an old rancher, Bill, a friend and drinking buddy of my father's, deep in the foothills of Alberta.

Chief was a wall-eyed, hammer-headed, ugly horse. But he was a horse. And I loved him just for that. He had a stance - legs stiff and rigid, ears back - that was how he met with the world. Bill questioned my father's sanity letting a mere girl ride 'that devil', as he called him. My father would reply that I would be just fine. He always said 'I would be just fine', about everything.

The horse never came when called, he always had to be caught (a bucket of oats, an old pickup, and Bill's roping skills). Bill would then saddle him for me (Chief spinning and humping his back), and bridle him (a bridle pieced together out of parts of an old bridle, binder twine, and a Spanish bit) and I would slip my foot into the stirrup and throw myself on to him. My father would then pull a bottle of rye whiskey out of his coat pocket and he and Bill would go to the house.

Bill would inevitably yell the same comment back to me every time:

"Stay away from the river! That there horse will toss you in it as sure as spitting on a dusty day."

"She'll be fine", my father said.

Then off Chief and I would go, me struggling the entire time to keep him to a pace less than a gallop. I've always said that Chief tried to kill me fifty different ways. And he did try to peel me off on every fence or tree he came to (but there were very few of either) and he tried a couple of times to roll with me in a few streams but it was kind of half-hearted, more a suggestion.

But, now that I think on it, it was Bill that he bucked off and into the bed of the truck, then kicked a couple of decent sized dents in the bed for good measure, Bill's head mere inches away. It was my father that he bit hard enough to break the bone in his finger. It was Bill's grown son, Jimmy, that he cornered in the barn and leaned on so hard that Jimmy passed out.

The only thing that Chief actually did to me that was scary was that he ran away with me once. But it was the middle of winter, the road that went past the ranch (that I rode on because the snow was too deep in the coulees) was icy and frequented by huge tractor-trailer trucks. We should never have been on it. So Chief took the bit in his teeth and took us home.

I grew to really love that horse. I wouldn't have realized it at the time but that horse was green broke if he was broke at all and had probably been abused a good deal. But I loved him.

I had him two years. And then my father *lost* him in another poker game. I sobbed for days. My father said stop crying. That I would be just fine.

Paintings

The sun and the snow are painting this morning.
Long shadows.
Smears of umbra, daubs of adumbration.
Glazing with light, spattering with glare,
a bit of sgraffito with the bushes and scrub.
Phthalo, prussian, and cerulean blues.
 I'm just curious as to who is going to sign in the bottom right-
hand corner.

Reflections on an Upside-Down World

There is a moss-covered fallen tree beside a puddle. And in that puddle, the world appears upside-down. Or, perhaps, that is the *real* world, there, in that puddle. And *we* are the reflection. Why not . . .

Thinking on that makes my head hurt. Makes me want to lay my head down on that soft, soft moss. Soft like a lap, soft like a breast.

Smelling of dust, smelling of moist, smelling of many small, small lives.

And have this world, this maybe world, stroke my back, hum a tuneless hum, and say:

"There, there, child. There, there."

Remember This

I woke remembering . . .

that I have sat with dragonflies,

have felt them traipse the geography of my body.

I have held a bird, like a kitten,

in my lap - quick timpani of fluttered heart beats

pulsing below my fingers.

I have seen the setting of the sun in an upturned face

and a woman dance with her bees.

I have stood at the edge of an entire ocean,

waves drinking at my naked feet,

swallowing everything that is left of me.

The Cat and the Pelican

The cat and the pelican watch the sun rise . . .

- from atop an old, beaten up dresser that has moved with us for at least 30 years . . .

- with one drawer filled with bicycle shorts from when riding in Italy; swimming suits from when we were thinner . . .

- beside a pile of clean, folded laundry, which is one of my favorite things . . .

-      clothes so well-worn and softened with age, they fold themselves into the remembered creases.

- beside a bowl of meditation balls that chime when you hold them, sing when you roll them . . .

- that are in a wooden bowl, carved of applewood; carved by a friend whose hands know the bowl the wood wants to be . . .

- the pelican carved by an ex-soldier, dogged by PTSD, to quiet his mind and delight his grandchildren . . .

-      the cat simply a Zen master, as all cats are; he has many, many toes . . .

April 1st

I wish I could speak of a morning's sunrise;
a horizon painted with silks -
azure and crystal blue and orange flame
and the pink of babies toes.

Instead, after a night of ear-lulling wind,
the great snow-eater,
the earth is bare and the windowpane
spattered with rain.

Appropriately so as today starts April,
April showers and all that.
But I don't trust April. I don't trust her one bit.
It will be bare arms today but wool socks tomorrow.

She can't help herself.

Linda H.Y. Hegland

The Dance

The dance in the night,
the one that swirls in the halls,
the foot stamping hard,
the old rhythm raw.
The animal dance, the dance
that hurts the old bones;
the step that is awkward
but finds its own grace.
The dance that is fierce,
hair flying wild, a mute
bay at the moon.
A nod to the ticking of
heat in the pipes that keeps
its own music, its own beat
in the night.
Hold the belly from laughing
to not wake the dog on the bed,
nor the man that sleeps too, the man
that is loved;
nor the cat that will come
slinking and chasing my step
of the dance in the hallway,
the dance in the night.

Botany Trip

I was on a botany field trip, up high on a mountain, in 1983.

Standing at the bottom of the trail that led up to Table Mountain was me, a 'mature' fine arts student, amongst about a dozen youngsters - all science students. It was a botany field trip wherein we would hike the 10 kilometre trail to the 'tourist' summit and then beyond to where the university had an alpine bunkhouse nestled in a mountain meadow, collecting specimens along the way.

The botany professor brought his psychologist wife. The professor was tall and scrawny, Ichabod-like with a lanky gait. His wife was short and round. She took a hurried three or four steps to his one. They held hands all the way to the top, only letting go when we came to the frequent fallen trees that lay across the trail. There, the professor's wife would scramble over to stand on top and insist on a kiss from the professor before she would slip down on the other side. Every time.

The professor had built an addition on to his home to house a variety of parasitic mistletoe. The plant was decades old and was immense. He visited it every day, sitting with it and talking with it, finally tipping the remains of his cup of tea onto it roots when he left. It was his life's work and his passion. The professor's wife collected eccentric, intelligent children - three of their own and two adopted - that she home-schooled, the house strewn with musical instruments and globes and easels and microscopes. Her patients and his students, both frequent visitors to the house, had to step over collected rocks, maneuver around guinea pigs, and avoid ricocheting children as they made their way to meetings with the professor or his wife. I have always thought those two defined love. And marriage.

One of the students was a First Nations man - very large, hair down to the middle of his back, face square. He lumbered along and every once in a while he would point out various things and tell us something about it, finishing with "my elders taught me that". Then he would get a glint in his eye and a bit of a smirk and follow up by saying "not really".

The first evening of the botany weekend at the bunkhouse and it was clear and warm. We built a bonfire and drank warm beer and too-sweet wine. One of the girls, a biology student, I knew from another class. She had given our boys two of the gerbils that she routinely 'saved' from the experimental lab. Though she had promised she would spay/neuter them that never happened and, instead, we struggled with aquarium tanks full of twenty-four gerbils, constantly trying to keep males and females apart, our boys having long since lost interest.

That bonfire night, she had found a guitar in the rafters. She tuned the guitar and it responded like it was an old friend. Then she sang 'Dust in the Wind' by Kansas - " . . . nothing lasts forever but the earth and sky . . . dust in the wind, all we are is dust in the wind". I have always loved that song. She sat in the dark and the sparks from the fire flew up and lit the strings on the guitar, the fireflies flittered around her head and lit her face, and above that the Milky Way spun slowly high in the sky. Like a spotlight on her raised face and her voice like a bell that chimed off of the cliffs.

The lake, that was clear to the bottom, held the moon in its waters.

Poets

In the stillness of tears
the poets sleep, dreaming of
souls below the light.
No words left -
like a dancer alone on the stage,
steps forgotten.
On those nights their hearts
grow unquiet; marvel
at the dread brokenness.
Longing to be found again;
to find again, perhaps by
going home in a different light.

March 1st

It is the first day of March. Icicles still adorn roof lines - singing water frozen mid-note. The air tastes of spilled stars.

There is that seam in March, that jagged line, that thin veil. And on the other side of that is where the warm-blooded gods begin to stir; where the air tastes of rot/birth; where the blood loosens.

Just waiting on that seam to tear.

The Sound of Rain

It's raining.

And I listened to it last night through the open bedroom window.

The sound it makes when it falls on the root cellar door below.

The sound it makes when it sluices off the ends of oak leaves.

The 'bacon sizzling in a frying pan' sound of a passing car.

Mostly it is a steady pattering lullaby and I slept well.

July

It is July. That time of sitting on the porch in the sultry but breezy afternoons, listening to the mourning doves. Hay-making season. Red sun-burned and wind-burned cheeks.

I knew a girl named July once. She came sometimes to the farm on which I spent my summers. She said that she had been born in a January, small and sickly and not ready for the world. The doctors had told her mother she would be dead by July. So her mother named her July, for the month in which she would leave.

And she didn't, of course, leave.

Each year we kids asked her:

"Are you dying *this* July?"

We weren't making fun or being macabre, we were truly curious. Would this be the year she lived up to her name? Would this be the July of her making and unmaking?

Then one year I asked her the question, not really caring about the answer, it was rote by now, and she slapped my face. Red cheeks in July.

Sound

This morning it is raining. Hard. Sheeting down; in my studio sounding like a ballroom of silk skirts.

In the bedroom, because of the heat of the night, the floor fan rotates back and forth, a whirr of small sound. But through the open window the sound of the rain and the wind enters the room, engulfs the whirr, flutters and punches at the place where the two winds meet - syncopated notes, strange looping music.

Like an Andrew Bird looped fiddle/violin piece - the notes and music repeated and layered on each other. A hypnotic, spiralling waterfall of notes and sound - like this morning's rain. I get lost in Bird's music.

Or like the time I was in the hoodoos in Alberta. Those strange, wind-carved formations. So silent, silent, except for the wind. The wind, that when it curls around and through the shapes makes music. Low moans and high whistles. Like an earth harp. The kind of sound you swallow whole.

Falcons and Falling Stars

We lay in a truck bed on a sultry summer night, under a slivered moon and a sky full of falling stars. Our seventeen-year-old selves, speaking of fate and wishes. Speaking of faithfulness and futures.

And you told me the story of a man that had caught a falcon, wild and vicious. And how he trained her to return to him, always return to him. First with the weight of chains and the tight bonds of leather, over and over, and over and over. Always pulled back. Always returning. Until finally the falcon only wore floating skeins of silk on her talons. But they were enough to bring her back, always, to the man. Disciplined and tamed.

And I held in my hand the letter you had written to me. About how we would marry at eighteen; about how we would have four children, two boys and two girls; about how we would winter in Florida; about how we would do everything and be everything - together.

And you squinted your eyes and held your hand in the air, catching stars and making them grant wishes. And each of those things in that letter you made into a wish. You held the stars tight until they flicked dark in your hands. Like a firefly doused.

And the tears that I wept ran from my eyes to my ears and lost themselves in my hair, as I stared up at that sky. And you thought they were tears of happiness.

But, in truth, I couldn't breathe.

You said the story of the bird was beautiful; that it told of faithfulness and of being true. But I thought that story was so sad, so very sad. To that broken-spirited bird, floating silk was as heavy as chains.

You wished to catch stars in your hands. Grasp them until they gave up their wishes. But I wanted the stars to follow their instincts. To fall freely, to immolate themselves in the skin of the sky, with passion.

The next day I told you to go away. The next day I broke your heart. Deliberately. You said. And the rumours on which small towns thrive said that you hated me. That I was faithless and untrue.

As capricious as a falcon's heart; as unstable as a dying star.

But, in truth, I just wanted to be a bird that flew free.

In truth, I just wanted to be a star that knew ecstasy.

Sweet, Sweet Burn of Summer

"sweet, sweet burn of sun and summer wind" ~ k.d. lang

Summer on the prairie pays no attention to things like sun screen. The sun is high and unimpeded by shade. It shines for long, interminable hours, white-bright and hot. Throughout the course of the summer the sun burned wide pink lines across my shoulders; new freckles across my nose. A wide strand of hair on each side of my face would turn bleached white. The thin skin at the tops of my ears peeled over and over.

When my mother washed my hair each week she would lay all the detritus the constant wind had woven into the strands, onto a dish at the side of the bath. Crisp leaves left over from winter, tiny twigs with sharp, tiny thorns, little feathered bits of old birds' nests, and wheat awns, *always* wheat. The water would turn black with dust.

I was so very upset when, at age 10, my mother started making me wear undershirts over my bare back and chest. She said I had to because I was a girl, though I still looked no different than the boys. I was sad and mad that the sun could no longer paint my back and shoulders with lines and shapes dependent on how fast I ran or how long I sat watching ants in the dirt. Its canvas covered.

And years later, in that summer sun and summer wind, a friend and I piling our boys into a garden wagon and hauling them down a long, long coulee to the river bottom to pick saskatoons. The wind tangled their hair into tumbleweeds. The day became so hot that even the shade under the berry bushes was too warm - under the bushes where the boys panted in the heat along with the occasional rabbit and once a lame grouse. So we would plonk the boys down in a low, fast stream, no wider than a foot, racing to the Oldman river, and show them how to make dancing bums (take off your underwear and place it underwater facing upstream, anchored with a couple of stones. The water fills the underwear and ta-da, dancing bums).

Mouths filled with juicy saskatoons. Hair filled with dust. Eyes filled with blue sky and bright sunshine. Wind scouring tears from our eyes.

Summer.

Early Hours of a Post-Tropical Storm

3:00 am. The rain and winds of post-tropical storm Elsa still batters at the house. When we went to bed I closed the bedroom windows as the drafts slammed doors shut throughout the house. At 2:00 am, I opened the windows again as it was hot and stifling. I let the wind back in.

The storm throws rain at the window and it sounds like the popcorn that spills out of those theatre hoppers - staccato. The wind mutters and then whines as it gusts; it inhales with a leaf-choked rattle and exhales with a breathy growl.

As I lay in bed I feel as the valley must feel as those gales blow through her, lifting her bullrush-hemmed skirts at the river banks, swirling the leaves of her trees until she can't bear the titillation. Just as I feel when the wind lifts the sheet from my hip and whispers up my back; or as it puffs a wisp of my hair across my cheek - carelessly. It does not leave me rest.

Wilding

Recently a friend returned a book I had lent him (Wilding by Isabella Tree). A heady read, a book of hope. I will re-read it at some time, I think. Or lend it again. We are trying to re-wild our land. And also trying to feed ourselves.

When we moved here there was already a huge variety of trees. And gradually we are adding more trees back to the land - trees that are native, trees for beauty, trees for food. The old man that lived here before us, Walter (for whom we named both our ghost and our cat) bought this piece of land because he recognized that here was a micro-climate. And he wanted to grow peaches. And, no, peaches are not a sort of re-wilding but the passion of an old Polish man (whose last name means grower of hops) who lived forever by himself, taking a walk up the road every day rain or shine or snow.

He planted peaches. And they have survived. Last year there were peaches on Walter's trees. They were small and gnarly and really quite ugly but they tasted exquisite. So not only will they stay (to honour a man who lived on loneliness and peaches), we have added more peach trees to Walter's peach trees. Perhaps they were lonely too.

So, too, have the birds come back. When we first came, our land was trim and tidy and mown to within an inch of its life (literally). Birdsong, but not a lot. Now our land is 'messy' and tumbled and verdant and the variety and number of birds has grown and grown. Every morning now sounds like an orchestra tuning up. From bass drum to triangle.

And the frogs and toads have come back. There is a boggy patch at the bottom of our Blueberry Hill where one of the springs flows under the hill. We planted a water garden there three years ago to try and deal with that. But it didn't work for a variety of reasons. So we pulled the plants out and just let it be. On rainy days it becomes particularly boggy. But it is lovely to stand outside the back door on a rainy, dark evening and hear some big bullfrog splashing about there like he is having a day at the spa. And to see smaller frogs hopping about at the edge of the dog yard.

We know snakes are back, too, because one stole eggs from out under our broody hen last year.

I have planted flowers over the last four years. Dug in the rocky, root-riddled soil to find places to plant flowers that attract birds and bees and butterflies and hummingbirds. No 'prima donna' flowers. With the exception of my roses, I suppose. Sometimes one plants something that holds no natural value but scent and memories. But even they have to hold their own.

So, we are trying, over time, to bring our land back and, in the process, cooperate with the land to grow gardens of edibles. It is ongoing, a work in progress. Helping the wild to find itself again here - out of the civility and concrete. As George Carlin said: "I like it when a flower or a little tuft of grass grows through a crack in the concrete. It's so fuckin' heroic."

Barefoot

As soon as the snow is gone from the porch, I am barefoot. Barefoot on the warm porch boards, barefoot in the dew-wetted grass, and barefoot in the house, always.

I do not have beautiful feet. A boy I knew loved my best friend because and only because she had beautiful feet. No one has ever worshipped *my* feet; my not beautiful feet.

My feet are thin and the toes twisted and tucked under a bit because of wearing shoes that were too small for too long when I was a child. The plight of most poor children, I would imagine, despite a father working two jobs.

And they are bony feet.

I like to think of my feet, throughout the barefoot times, growing, like the soil, layers of clay and moss and callouses. A patina of sunburn and scratches and red dust. My mother would insist that I wash the prairie and the creeks and the grasses off my feet every night. So as not to dirty the bedsheets.

Now, I don't always remember to do that. But the sheets are my own and I don't mind taking the dust and grass to bed with me. And sometimes a tiny twig caught in the twisted toes.

Rum and Blowing Glass

This morning is dull-skied, a bit windy, cool but you can feel the humidity in the air. The sun is already looking a little intense as it bites through the fog. By this afternoon it will be 'feels like' 32 C. Like a foundry.

When we were living in Illinois we took our boys to an open house at the art school. It was the glass-making foundry. It was set up in an old, cavernous barn. Huge black ovens lined the walls; huge vats of water all up and down the barn.

Red flames licked from the ovens and the air was filled with steam from the dousing of hot glass. It was fascinating watching the large colourful globs of volcano-hot, liquid glass spin on the end of long poles. It was fascinating watching the intensity on the faces of almost all bearded, all long-haired, all bare-chested glassblowers; all with burn scars up and down their arms. One son thought they looked like a Viking village; the other son thought Lord of the Rings. It would not have been unusual to see a dragon curled in the corner, sleeping on glowing coals.

At one point one of the men offered our boys huge chunks of rum cake. The boys each took one bite and spit it out. I tried a bite and it near burned the tongue out of my mouth. There was so much rum poured over the cake that, literally and without exaggeration, you could have wrung out that piece of cake and filled a glass with rum. If you had taken a piece close to one of the ovens it would have ignited.

I thought then that the jovial and almost careless way the glassblowers moved in and around each other, pushing molten glass into ovens, pulling it out and spinning it wildly in the air, dousing it in water, filling the air with steam, was a little 'off'. Several rum cakes dotted the tables around the edges of the barn. The glassblowers downed huge chunks like they were swigs of water.

I think they may all have been just a little drunk. But I have been told that glassblowers are a little crazy anyway. Playing with volcanoes and lava and scalding steam.

Horses at Bozeman

In 1983, when my eldest son was seven and my youngest was two, we travelled to visit a friend's mother in Bozeman, Montana. Early on the wintry Sunday morning, my eldest ran down to the pasture where three horses grazed, punching holes in the snow with their hooves to get at the grass. He wouldn't come back for breakfast so I quickly pulled on a coat and boots, hefted my youngest to my hip, and went down too. My sons had been promised a walk/ride on the horses and the excitement went beyond waiting for breakfast or real light.

The horses were large and shaggy. Their manes were long dreadlocks and, still held in their tangle, bits of grasses and weeds, vines and thistles. A promise, here in the middle of winter, of summer that was and spring that will be.

My sons rode bareback, their cold hands buried in thick hair, and my friend and I led the horses by their halters. Up into woods, down by a stream that still ran and bubbled below ice, through drifts of snow to our knees. The mountains loomed winter-cold. The sun was a dull greyness in the sky and, as the day wore on, we only knew it was approaching evening by the deepening chill.

My friend and I told my boys stories as we trudged through the winter day. About the mythical people and creatures of forests and fields. About the fortune-telling abilities of owls. About how wolves sing the sorrows of the world.

At one point my youngest fell asleep, his face buried in those dreadlocks, and my eldest said he wanted a song.

So we sang Michael Martin Murphey's 'Wildfire':

"She comes down from Yellow Mountain
On a dark, flat land she rides
On a pony she named Wildfire
With a whirlwind by her side
On a cold Nebraska night
Oh, they say she died one winter
When there came a killing frost
And the pony she named Wildfire
Busted down its stall
In a blizzard, he was lost
She ran calling Wildfire
She ran calling Wildfire
She ran calling Wildfire . . . "

The Salinger Man

The field of hay that has been growing taller as my walks have grown longer is cut now. There was a fellow by a tractor about to put his two dogs - a big rangy pointer and a little yappy Toto dog up into the cab. The dogs saw me and came running to see me. The fellow, young, bearded, with a farmer's peaked hat down over his brow, sauntered over to fetch them back. We talked.

He told me that he liked the company of them in the cab. That he had an old, very slow square baler and that it would take him all day and into the evening, until it was too dark to see, to get this field done before the rains this week. That the dogs would keep him company for a bit of time. At least until they wanted out to chase the hares the baler scared up.

He said that he reads to fill the time as he slowly slowly chugs up one row and down another, looking up at the mountain occasionally to watch for hawks or turkey vultures drifting on the thermals. He drives with his knees and reads until the light fades. I asked him what he reads. He held the book out to me. Salinger.

Wild Geese

We took my two sons to a little zoo/wildlife centre when we lived in Illinois. The boys found it quite confusing that there were Canada Geese in a fenced enclosure.

Their experience of Canada geese to that point had been sitting out in the backyard of our house in Alberta and watching a wavering V of geese, quite low, beating their way down to the river, talking and gossiping; garrulous honks. The wings thrumming and creaking.

On that river, flowing slow and thick, my sons often sat piling rocks on the banks while the geese bobbed with brown pelicans out on the water. *These* Canada geese, that came to the fence to accept grass and reeds offered by grubby boy-fingers, had their wings clipped. As caged as any zoo animal is. No rising en masse on hardy wings to heed a call. No river-wetted feet.

It was a sad day, that day we met geese, as one of the boys said, "with their wild all gone".

Oslo

I unearthed a notebook today. From 2015. Oslo, Norway.

We had wandered the streets of Oslo all day, wandering up and down little streets, avoiding tourists. On the way back to the hotel, we wandered over to the docks, scouting out where our overnight ferry would be leaving from the next day.

Just as we were returning from the port, I took a bad fall – smashing my knee and cutting my face. We slowly (due to my hobbling) made our way back to the hotel. Our strolling was done for the day. With ice packed on my knee, numbed with pain killers and wine, and eating the sandwiches we had picked up earlier in the day, we watched the BBC (about the only station we could understand). And later the Eurovision competition.

The next day we had reservations to see the phenomenal Opera and Ballet House, across the street from our hotel. I was in no shape to be climbing up and down stairs, or hobble along on marble floors so I convinced Bar to go by himself and I stayed behind. He helped settle me in the foyer of the hotel and I made myself comfortable with a pillow, a cappuccino (constantly refilled by the staff) and my notebook – quite happy with a morning of people watching. And *this* is why I love people watching. I wrote down every word of his conversation:

A man from Nairobi approached the front desk near where I was sitting, to check out.

"Thank you for hosting me," he said to the clerk. "I had a most wonderful experience, you are nice people.

But I am missing home. Home is where all of me is. Home is where I can wear my feet bare in the dust."

He laughed self-deprecatingly.

"But thank you again for hosting me. Your country, Norway, is very green and fresh. But I am used to different colours. Good bye, kwaheri."

Old Trucks and Prairie Songs

Dust rises behind the pickup as I drive across the prairie, along the grooves that run deep and permanent across it – originally made by wagon wheels hundreds of years earlier. Scars. Gophers watch from their mounds, whistling piercing notes of warning before upending themselves into their holes, disappearing from sight with the flick of a black-tipped tail. The truck is a 1965 dust-grayed GMC with standard drive and windows you have to crank manually. One window drops with a glassy thud a third of the way down; the other sticks on every turn. Once you get it down, you leave it down.

I am helping friends bring in their hay. I drive slowly along and others heft the bales into the back of the truck. Each load I drive back to the barn, where others lift the bales into the hayloft. I am driving back over the prairie after my last load. I wear an old denim shirt with sleeves rolled up to the elbows, worn jeans, my hair tied up in a messy, grimy ponytail. Occasionally I spit the dust in my mouth out the window. You can't be a lady on the prairie. The prairie is embodied in me – in the way I dress, the way I move, the way I don't think twice about spitting out the truck window while I wrestle with its gears and stubbornness.

My two boys love riding in this truck. The vast, slippery vinyl seat invites shoving and horse-play. The window has a wide ledge and they hang their bellies over it, making themselves dizzy staring at the ground moving below. When they pull back into the truck their faces are as dust-grubby as the truck itself. But now they have fallen asleep in the dozy late afternoon sun, piled into the corner of the seat like fagged puppies. Their hair sticks out at sweaty angles; there is a burnished redness to their cheeks, an extra freckle or two on their noses. Their lips are parched.

I stop the truck at the top of a small knoll where there is an ancient medicine wheel. Though the prairie is dry and juiceless, the grasses around the stones are green. I remember that most prairie grass species have exceedingly long root systems. The roots are thin but some go as deep as fifteen feet to find moisture and richer soil. I recite the names of grasses, like a chant, a hymn. The grasses speak of other prairie creatures, of climate and soil:

   beak grass, bluestem, bottlebrush, buffalo grass, porcupine grass, brome,

     satin grass, panic grass, rattlesnake grass, riverbank wild rye, sand

     dropseed, side oats gama, sweet grass (oh ambrosial, worshipped

          Sweetgrass!), switch grass

As I sit, eyes closed, dust caked in my nostrils and sweat trickling down my back, I listen to the prairie symphony – the whirr of grasshoppers, the high whining keen of the shortgrass, birdsong low and high, gopher whistles, hawk shrieks . . .

   blue-winged teal, killdeer, avocet, red-winged blackbird, great-horned owl,

     chestnut-collared longspur, whooping crane, saltmarsh sharp-tailed

     sparrow, meadow lark (just seven notes!), magpie, Swainson's

     hawk, three-toed woodpecker, peregrine falcon, marbled

     godwit, brown pelican, burrowing owl

The conductor is the thrum, thrum of the prairie wind,

Chinook wind,

Foehn wind,

rain shadow wind.

Wind textures, insect medleys, birdsong choir. We are enduringly in 'place'. We are immersed in places, always at one latitude or another, and intimately caught up in the natural ambience around us.

***

When I revisit a place that had significance in a past phase of my life, as when I returned to the prairie to bury my father's ashes, I take a moment to consider my present self with the one that inhabited that place years ago. Sometimes I lament the arc that took me from that place. But, if I were to be honest, this lamentation is steeped in nostalgia and poignancy. The prairie place I knew then no longer exists. That wild prairie of my past is all but gone – plowed under massive fields of grain or grazed to dust by herds of cattle. Barbed wire creates quilts of tamed squares of land. That place has disappeared under hundreds of houses, big box stores, and a prison - existing only in my imagination and memories. Though I will never forget the land, it appears to have forgotten me.

On that trip to bring my father home, I asked my brother to drive me out to the prairie – where he himself often travels, alone, with a thermos of whiskey-laced coffee, old rock-and-roll on the radio. He seeks ancient, slumping barns and abandoned rusting Harvesters to take pictures of. We drove and drove. That prairie in which my sons first began their unfolding to the experience of place, is ebbing and diminishing out from the edges of the town. We did finally find it, but it took a good few miles and time.

We pulled into a field, drove to the edge of a coulee, turned the engine off. As we sat in my brother's truck, with the sound of the ticking engine and the occasional grasshopper clacking against the grill making a sort of contrapuntal music, I gazed. Falling in love with that place was not something I imagined I'd ever do. But I wanted to take the time to at least accept it - the impact the years I spent on the prairie had on my life.

Scratchings on paper in the middle of the night, scribbles on envelopes left deep in pockets, sketch of a bird in the holly tree, two lines of a poem about the wind. They are all mere twitchings of nature, of my searching for place. I yearn to be feral; I wish to haunt rivers, to run with antelope along the creases of the coulees. I long to sleep un-bedded beneath the star-pocked sky and wake hung with dew. I ache for that place to remember me. Because it's the wind I miss most, now that it's gone.

Place of Ocean – Tides and Heartbeats

Me, a prairie girl, to the ocean,
Pacific, for the first time
on the far west side
of a west coast island.

The sand on the beach
hard, unyielding.
I had expected to
curl my toes in soft sand
like the pictures in travel magazines.

The sand reached distant and grey
to the fog, marine mist.
I crimped my feet over its ridges,
crease after crease,
ran my tongue round bony palate of my mouth;
the same.

A roar that gorged my ears,
punctuated with bird call, screech.
I drew closer to the fog, the brume
like tinsel tears
in my hair.

Booming waves that galloped into shore,
taller than me, before they fell and shoved
themselves turbulently against the sand,
puddling and foaming, seashells and driftwood.

the sea wind dragged my hair.
the water churned round my ankles.

Pulling back to the ocean
the waves gulped the breath from me,
sucked at the blood in my veins.
I would have followed
but my earth-logged feet
remained moored in the seaweed,
clasping me to shore.

Kissing Rabbits

My granddad was a bare-knuckle boxer. Behind English pubs and in night-muted limestone quarries, he fought all comers. His face bore the cragginess of fractured cheekbones and a shattered nose. He learned his craft from the gypsies that camped on his land. They earned their pasture keep by tending to his draft horses and his pit ponies. And each time they came, they took his measure in fights that marked his face anew and crippled his knuckles.

Once.

Granddad spoke little; was sparse with affection. But, in his taciturn manner, he played guessing games with me about what the weather would bring, or on which side of the oak tree the moss would grow heaviest, or how many kittens the old she-cat would have (fewer and fewer each year). He once took my hand and we followed and watched as one of the old, lame gypsy dogs wandered into the forest, laid down after turning and turning – and quietly died; its legs stretching with toes like starbursts and its lips curling back from its teeth. Granddad's world, and what he showed me of it, was secluded but brimful, meagre but exquisite.

Once.

My granddad came out from the stone barn. His hands were bloodied and small drifts of tender fur clung to his hair and his clothing. When his back was turned, I peered hesitantly in at the door of the barn. Several small, bloody carcasses were piled on a bench. Next to them was a pile of skins. In the pens lining the walls, rabbits thumped and bumped and wiggled noses at me.

Over time, I had learned the measure of my granddad. I knew him to be a hard man, aloof, a hard and constant drinker, a man of puzzle and contradictions. He went about the job of slaughtering his rabbits with skill and speed – a perfunctory chore in the course of his day. But I had hidden in the hayloft once – consumed by a morbid curiosity. I watched as my granddad selected the rabbit, as he lifted it from the pen; how he sat with the rabbit facing away from him. I was prepared to squeeze my eyes shut and cover my mouth so I didn't scream. But gently, Granddad lifted the rabbit to his lips and kissed it, tenderly and sadly, on the top of its head. Then, so quickly that I missed it, he snapped the rabbit's neck and laid it limply across his lap. All I heard was a faint 'click'.

Over and over, Granddad did the same – every rabbit kissed, killed, and skinned. Both rabbits and death mute.

Once.

Night, and the gypsies in their camp danced with the fire and played their sweet, wild music to the moon. And on this night, I crept from my bed – drawn by the music and the swirling shadows made large and dreadful by the firelight - and hid in the loft of the barn. Granddad had gone to the pub, I thought, as he did every night; striding along the rutted road, his long arms swinging at his side, his fight-scarred hands like hammers at the end of them. I knew he would not return until that hour of the early morning when the wind quickened and owl-hoot turned to the twitter of wrens that hid amongst the gorse and sang the sun up.

But at this hour the night was warm, the dark of the stone barn was soft as velvet and as close as my own heartbeat – beating hard with the pulse of the leather drums, blood racing through it with the searing wail of the fiddles. As my eyes grew accustomed to the dark, as my excitement calmed, I was able to savour the details of the scene before me - the leaping flames, the soft-lit lanterns hanging from the ends of caravans, the two dogs tussling over a well-gnawed bone. My eyes saw the old man playing the fiddle, the broken horsehairs hanging from the frets like fine thistledown. I saw a woman serenely spinning around the fire, a baby in her arms and a small naked child clinging to her skirts. I saw a group of men passing a large, ceramic bottle amongst them, and amongst themI saw my granddad.

He was hunched over himself, his arms draped over his knees. His head drooped as though it were too heavy for his neck and his maimed hands twitched. The bottle continued to be passed back and forth. A man rose and stood in front of Granddad. He stared down at him, took the bottle from him and drunk, the liquid dribbling down his chin. He was an old man, with dirty feet and a weeping, rheumy eye. He grabbed Granddad by the neck of his shirt and pulled him to his feet with an unexpected strength. My granddad rocked on his feet, stumbled forward towards the old man, fists clenched, his eyes hardening.

The others around the campfire started clapping, the women ululated. As the drums slowed to a blood-paced beat, Granddad started swaying – the old man released his hold and stepped away. The swaying took on purpose, the movement started to understand the music. Granddad raised his arms and I thought of the willow down by the steam, its dangling arms stirring eddies into the stream, just as my granddad's fingers stirred the stars in the sky. He started taking mincing steps around the fire and, now and then, dipped towards it – close, close – then reared back and spun away. Then he stopped and weaved with his arms raised. A young girl, with bare legs and a gold tooth that shone in the firelight, poked his ribs and stroked his face. His expression never changed – his face stone and rigid, deep frown lines between his brows. But eventually he closed his eyes, swaying and turning, and he looked . . . peaceful.

Once.

And I knew dismay sharper than that of dead rabbits.

Loving Monsters

Over the course of this summer, late at night past midnight or in the early hours of three am, the crickets chirr to a halt and the night chorus of the coywolves begins. It starts with murmurs and ascends into hysterical yips and yaps, and finally rounds into full-throated howls that make your heart thud. There is nothing like laying in bed under civilized bamboo sheets and feeling the responsive tingle that begins in your toes and exits through the top of your head—your body and mind on a high-tension wire plucked by the wild sounds.

Nocturnal laments. Lunar lullabies.

We have recently moved to this farm on the side of a mountain in Nova Scotia. We had only been living at our farm for a few weeks when the nightly songs began. When first I heard them, I thought—coyotes. But the sound was not solitary nor soprano like that of the prairie coyote of my experience. As the sound became that of multiple beings and the tone deepened to mournful long howls I thought - wolves. Then a neighbouring farmer told me of the coywolf—a large hybrid coyote/wolf sometime mixed with dog, that has become common to the area around our wild farm.

They come down from the mountain behind us and up from the valley to run the moon paths across the fields or along the trails where the railway tracks have been pulled up. The sound of them echoes off the basalt walls of the slope. I sometimes find scat in the yard close to the house. And on our walks after a rainy night I find their enormous paw prints in the disused road.

When they sing their night-time canticles, the local dogs whine and call out over the wind themselves. They sense the wild. It calls to them and, if they are chained, they pull at their tethers and chew at their feet, feeling that same wire that I feel, vibrating in their bones and blood. Dogs can be full of heartache and poetry too and dream of running, full-throated.

I know, in my human scientific mind, that coyotes and wolves and our resident coywolves do not actually howl at the moon. They will ululate and keen whether there is a moon out or not. But I know of a wolf that missed the moon. He lived his entire life in a zoo. His enclosure was concrete, the bars were heavy and rusted, and at night he was shut away in a roofed ghetto where not a single glint of starlight fell through the cement ceiling, let alone moonbeams. Every weekend of my childhood living in that city I went to the zoo and sat by the wolf's cage. He was already very old. The keeper loved to tell all who would listen about the oddity of this wolf - he never howled. Not ever.

That wolf lived to be 27 years old. Never howled. Never followed nor sang along a lane of light. The keeper boasted of how it was the fact that the wolf was captive that he lived so long—that if he had been left wild, he would have died after a short life. I think, maybe, lives of misery and restlessness and sadness are very long lives. Lives of bliss are short.

I remember another experience of wolves. We were camping with our two small boys, waiting for a meteor shower; so, we were up very late, high in the mountains, with only the night sky for illumination. Around our camp the darkness was deep, and beside our camp the river ran heavy and turbulent; our ears so acclimated to the sound of it running to the ocean that it was mere ambience.

Laying on our backs, we waited for the meteor shower. We guessed at which were planets, which were stars, and which were satellites spinning endlessly until they died.

Sputnik. Asteroid. Moon.

The meteorites began streaking across the night-fallen sky. One, then two, then twenty. Then, un-countable. They spoke, those meteorites. The fizzle of a flame. The swish of ladies' skirts. The sibilance of snakes. The whisper of vast rocks dying in the sky.

And out of the woods came the shadows of wolves. The pant-gutter sound of pursuit. The innuendo of foot-falls. The murmuring secret of them. They stood, just for a moment, and looked our way. The gold-flecked feral yellow of wolves' eyes in the moon-soaked night. And, just for a moment—with tumbling river, and sizzling skies, and silent taciturn forest about us . . . . we were wild too.

My sons barely breathed. I felt the fluttering tremble of my youngest son's heart as he leaned back against me. It went from his chest, through his back, to my chest. Like that high-tension wire, plucked and thrumming—tingling, a shiver.

I think of that sometimes when I lay in bed at night, listening, and I think of that moon-starved wolf too. And I think of wide-eyed young lads under star-spilled skies feeling that same pull at something deep behind their bellies—just like the neighbour's fettered dog.

It doesn't matter if they are coyotes, or wolves, or coywolves—or for that matter small boys in the dark trying to tell fireflies from falling stars. What matters is that they all know how to find the wakes left by moonlight . . . and how to sing the untamed and weeping notes of the truly wild.